DEC 2 2 2011

155.632
BASEN
GOT
Basen, Ryan.
Got your back : dealing with
friends and enemies
Essential health: a guy's guide

D0929186

DISCARDED
HURON PUBLIC LIBRARY

HURON PUBLIC LIBRARY
521 DAKOTA AVE S
HURON, SD 57350

YA
155.632
Bas

A GUY'S GUIDE

Got Your Back

Dealing with Friends and Enemies

ABDO
Publishing Company

HURON PUBLIC LIBRARY
521 DAKOTA AVE S
HURON, SD 57350

A GUY'S GUIDE

Got Your Back

Dealing with Friends and Enemies

by Ryan Basen

Content Consultant
Dr. Robyn J. A. Silverman
Child/Teen Development Expert and Success Coach
Powerful Words Character Development

Credits

Published by ABDO Publishing Company, 8000 West 78th Street, Edina, Minnesota 55439. Copyright © 2011 by Abdo Consulting Group, Inc. International copyrights reserved in all countries. No part of this book may be reproduced in any form without written permission from the publisher. The Essential Library™ is a trademark and logo of ABDO Publishing Company.

Printed in the United States of America,
North Mankato, Minnesota
062010
092010

 THIS BOOK CONTAINS AT LEAST 10% RECYCLED MATERIALS.

Editor: Rebecca Rowell
Copy Editor: Nick Cafarelli
Interior Design and Production: Marie Tupy
Cover Design: Marie Tupy

Library of Congress Cataloging-in-Publication Data
Basen, Ryan.
  Got your back : dealing with friends and enemies / Ryan Basen.
    p. cm. — (Essential health: a guy's guide)
  Includes index.
  ISBN 978-1-61613-540-9
  1. Friendship—Juvenile literature. 2. Interpersonal relations—Juvenile literature. 3. Boys—Psychology—Juvenile literature. I. Title.
  BF575.F66B367 2011
  155.6'32—dc22
                    2010017072

contents

Meet Dr. Robyn

Dr. Robyn Silverman truly enjoys spending time with young people. In fact, it's what she does best! As a child and teen development specialist, Dr. Robyn has devoted her career to helping guys just like you become all they can be—and possibly more than they ever imagined. Throughout this series, you'll read her expert advice on friends, girls, classmates, school, family, and everything in between.

A self-esteem and body image expert, Dr. Robyn takes a positive approach to life. She knows how tough it is to be a kid in today's world, and she's prepared with encouragement and guidance to help you become your very best and realize your goals.

Dr. Robyn helps young people share their wildest dreams and biggest problems. Her compassion, openness, and honesty make her trusted by many adolescents, and she considers it a gift to be able to interact with the young people whom she sees as the leaders of tomorrow. She created the Powerful Words Character Development system, a program taught all over the world in martial arts and other sports programs to help guys just like you become examples to others in their communities.

As a speaker, success coach, and award-winning author, Dr. Robyn's powerful messages have reached thousands of people. Her expert advice has been featured in *Prevention* magazine, *Parenting* magazine, *U.S. News and World Report*, and the *Washington Post*. She was an expert for *The Tyra Show*, *Fox News*, and NBC's *LXtv*. She has an online presence, too. You can follow her on Twitter, become a fan on Facebook, and read her blog on her Web site, www.DrRobynSilverman.com. When she isn't working, Dr. Robyn enjoys spending time with her family in New Jersey.

Dr. Robyn believes that young people are assets to be developed, not problems to be fixed. As she puts it, "Guys are so much more than the way the media paints them. They have so many things to offer. I'm ready to highlight how guys get it right and to provide tips for the ways they can make their teen years the best years so far . . . I'd be grateful if you'd come along for the ride."

You're at a great time in your life. Many people my age would gladly change positions with you. That's because you're about to start some great friendships. I still keep in touch with many of the kids I grew up with. This is one thing that's great about being a guy: Many of us have lifelong friendships.

But forming and maintaining these friendships isn't always easy. It wasn't for me, and you'll likely have your share of ups and downs, too. This book is full of stories about guys like you who experience problems getting along with other kids. These anecdotes touch on dealing with bullies, being a bully, being the new kid, being a loner, trying to fit in, and much more. You may have dealt with similar situations already. The good news is that by dealing with the drama, you will emerge a more mature and tested guy. And you will have friends you can rely on.

I know I did. Like most of the guys I grew up with, I can relate to every chapter in this book. I remember the loneliness and anxiety I felt when I switched schools, moving away from my friends. I can recall being targeted by bullies as a young middle school student because I was unsure about how to stand up for myself. I also regret the times in my early teen years when I found myself on the other side and acted like a bully. I laugh now when I think about all the fads my friends and I dove into. We were so eager to try on labels and fit in with the popular crowd.

I had a typical adolescence for an American guy, and I made it through. Hopefully, reading this book can help you flourish, too. Then, when you get to be an adult, you'll have a trustworthy, loyal group of friends of your own. You might reflect on the tough times you had during your adolescence and be glad you went through it all—and you might even smile and laugh about some of it. Because despite all of the drama, it will make you all better friends.

Good luck!

Ryan

1

The Loner

Making friends might come easily to you. You may have many friends and spend a lot of time with them. Perhaps you hang out with your friends several times a week or see each other every day in school. You spend the rest of the time with your family. So, maybe you don't know what it's like to be alone.

Some boys know that lonely feeling, though. For some reason, they don't click with other kids at school, at camp, or at extracurricular activities such as sports or band. Even after spending hours around other kids, they don't become friends with any of them. They are loners.

Being a loner is no fun. Few kids, if any, would choose not to have any friends. Even the shiest guys try to make friends. But they aren't always successful. They hang out by themselves and study by themselves. As a result, they feel isolated.

Jake was one such loner. Check out his experience to see how he handled going to school without any friends.

Jake's Story

Like all of his fifth grade classmates at his elementary school, Jake graduated in June and prepared to move to a new school. Unlike his peers, though, Jake had a few friends, but not many. He preferred to play video games and sometimes even board games by himself.

Jake's new middle school freaked him out. He was used to attending a school with about 100 kids in his grade. He knew many of them because he had been going to school with them for years. Jake's middle school, however, had 300 kids in the sixth grade. He didn't know most of his classmates.

At the start of the school year, many of Jake's old classmates continued hanging out with each other. But, just as had been the case in elementary school, Jake didn't hang out with them. And he felt weird starting conversations with kids he didn't know.

> Being a loner is no fun. Few kids, if any, would choose not to have friends.

HURON PUBLIC LIBRARY
521 DAKOTA AVE S
HURON, SD 57350

He could hear them talking as he walked by in the hall. A guy would say, "Hey, do you have Mr. Ash for math?"

"Yeah," the other guy would say, and just like that, two kids would become instant friends.

Other kids didn't reach out to Jake, either. Jake felt as if he didn't fit in with any of his classmates. He wasn't a great athlete. He wasn't in the school band. He didn't want to join any clubs. He was a good student, but he couldn't find anything in common with his peers outside of class.

Jake often ate lunch in the school cafeteria by himself or sat with teachers. During free times in gym class, he would shoot baskets by himself. Jake studied by himself, too. He did so even during study hall, when students were allowed to work together.

Think About It

· Why did Jake have trouble adjusting to his new school? Why do you think Jake avoided conversations with other kids?

· Have you ever felt too intimidated to approach other kids? Why did you feel that way?

· Have you seen a lonely student in your school? Have you tried to reach out to him?

Jake couldn't work by himself forever, though. One day in social studies, Mr. Murray announced, "For your oral reports on Australia, I am dividing you into groups. Lissy, Jamie, Zach, and Jake will be in our first group."

Jake felt a shiver go through his body when Mr. Murray said his name. Jamie immediately took charge. "Jake, what section do you want to do?" he asked. Jake paused. He knew nothing about Australia.

"Let's see," Jamie said, "I have Sydney already. How about Melbourne?"

"Uh, okay," Jake replied.

Jake dove into the assignment with the solid work ethic he applied to all his schoolwork. The group decided to meet at Jamie's house. Jake was nervous about meeting outside of school. What would he say to Jamie when he got to the door? What would the others say to him? What would they think of his part of the report?

The group gathered at Jamie's house that weekend. When it was Jake's turn to share his portion of their presentation, he delivered a detailed, five-minute speech about Melbourne. Jamie, Zach, and Lissy thought it was great. They had assumed Jake wouldn't really participate, so they were surprised he had been so well prepared.

what would the others say to him? what would they think of his part of the report?

"Wow, Jake. That was sick!" Jamie exclaimed.

"Um . . . thanks," he said, feeling his face flush.

"We're going to ace this report," Jamie said.

"Yeah, I hope so," Jake said.

The group presented their Australia report the next Monday in class. Jake did an excellent job, just as he had done at Jamie's house. The rest of the group also did well, and they received an A. The kids in the group were impressed with Jake. The rest of the kids seemed impressed, too.

That afternoon in gym class, Jake was shooting baskets by himself as usual. Jamie walked over and began shooting with him.

"So," Jamie said, "what's your deal? Like, what elementary school did you go to? Do you play a lot of basketball?"

Jake was surprised that someone wanted to know about him. "Uh, I went to Beverly Farms," he said. "I don't play much basketball. Football is my favorite sport."

"Cool," Jamie responded. "I play football all the time. Me and Cory and Zach, we usually play after school on Friday. Do you wanna play with us this week?

"Uh," Jake said. "Um. Okay. Yeah, cool."

Think About It

- Why was Jake nervous about meeting with his group outside of school?

- Why do you think Jake was able to ace his part of the report, especially when he'd been so shy about doing a group project?

- Why do you think Jamie started talking to Jake and invited him to play football? How do you think Jake feels about Jamie's invitation?

- Has a classmate ever reached out to you when you felt alone?

Jake accepted the invitation, but he was really nervous. He went to the park after school on Friday. He had butterflies in his stomach as he got to the park and saw about two dozen kids he barely knew. Although he wasn't great at football, he was decent enough to play. He caught a couple of passes and made a few tackles.

Most of the guys didn't know Jake. They only knew him as the kid who often shot baskets by himself in gym class. After the football game, though, they came over and talked with him.

"You're pretty good," Zach said. "I hope you're on my team next time." Then, Jamie came up to Jake. "Hey dude," he said. "You're in my math class too, right?

"Yeah, I think so," Jake replied.

"We have that test on Monday. You wanna come over and study for it on Sunday?" Jamie said.

This time, Jake did not hesitate to give an answer. "Sure, that'd be great" he said. "Let me know what time I should be there."

As Jake walked home from the park after the game, he smiled to himself and took a deep breath. He still was not entirely comfortable at his new school. He still felt too shy to approach many of his classmates. But he no longer felt isolated. Some of his classmates had noticed him and tried to get to know him. They seemed to like him and wanted to hang out with him. Maybe they would even become friends.

Think About It

- Why was Jake still a bit apprehensive about his new friends as he walked home?

- Have you ever reached out and tried to befriend a loner? What happened? Did you become friends?

- What about students who have an even harder time fitting in than Jake? How might you help them feel less alone?

- Do you think Jake will continue to hang out with Jamie and the other guys? Why or why not?

Being a loner can be difficult, but it isn't unusual. Hundreds of kids Jake's age don't feel like they mesh well with others. Sometimes, other kids avoid them because they may be viewed as quirky, weird, or simply different. They are different. Everybody is.

Many kids are too independent or too stubborn to feel comfortable in a group. Some are naturally introverted and reserved. So, it's easier for them to be alone. Others may prefer to cling to a parent or another adult, such as a teacher. Kids like Jake are often afraid of other kids—afraid of being judged, rejected, or treated poorly. So, they avoid them.

This is not healthy, though. Kids who don't have any people they can call close friends are at risk of depression. They are also more likely to drop out of school, be bullied, bully others, or use drugs. They could have a tougher time adjusting to adulthood. It's important for loners to work through their insecurities and be around other kids. Eventually, they will feel more comfortable and begin to open up. So, if you see a guy who is a loner, don't be afraid to be the one to take the first step. You might make a truly great friend.

Work It Out

1. Reach out to other kids who have interests similar to yours. Each time you reach out to someone, it will become easier the next time, until you no longer feel stressed about it. Connecting with others can make you feel more valued and understood.

2. Talk to your parents, a guidance counselor, or a school psychologist. Adults may have good ideas about how you can open up and meet new people.

3. Avoiding other kids may make you feel safe now, but being socially excluded and ignored can make you feel awful. Ignoring that feeling won't make it go away.

The Last Word from Ryan

Not all guys are the same. While some are really outgoing, others are shy and anxious around other people. These are natural traits, but that's not an excuse for avoiding others. Sometimes, being a loner just feels better— you don't have to deal with people. It can be difficult to make friends if you're shy. Don't give up. Don't avoid group projects, sports teams, and school clubs. Join them to pursue your own interests. Before long, you won't be a loner—and you won't want to be.

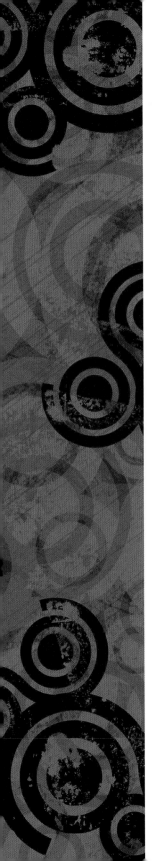

2
Mr. Popular

sk any adult if they were popular when they were your age. Many will laugh. Others will shudder. Still others will get nostalgic. Popularity is not as important to most adults. Many of them are even embarrassed that they considered their popularity to be so important when they were kids. Yet, that's just the way it is. Being popular is important to most kids your age.

Being popular is so important, in fact, that some guys get carried away with it. These guys make decisions based on how they think other kids will react to them. They might go out of their way to stay on top of rumors. They want to go to every dance or party. And when they become popular, they are sometimes mean to kids who aren't popular because they think that it will make them look better in the eyes of the other popular kids. They sometimes forget who they really are—and who their real friends are—and act like someone they really aren't.

Sean was one of those popular kids. Tall, good-looking, and athletic, Sean quickly became popular at camp one summer. Take a look at Sean's story for a lesson about being Mr. Popular.

Sean's Story

Sean jogged over to the sideline, grabbed his bottle of Gatorade, and took a big gulp. He wiped his forehead with his sleeve. He was playing a pickup basketball game on this first day of summer camp.

"Hi, Sean," he heard a girl call out.

Sean turned around and saw Ashley. She was a tall, brown-haired girl he had known for a couple years but had rarely talked to.

"Hey," he replied. She's hot, he thought.

Ashley smiled and continued walking past the court with a few friends.

Sean had been attending the same camp for a few years. He knew a lot of the kids there, but he had never thought

Being popular is so important that some guys get carried away with it. They make decisions based on how they think other kids will react to them.

much about being popular until the summer he turned 13. Suddenly, playing sports and working at the camp radio station weren't the only things Sean cared about. He now paid attention to girls and was desperate for them to notice him. He also wanted other guys to think he was cool.

Sean didn't know why being popular was suddenly important. He just knew that it was. This urge influenced every decision he made, from what shorts to wear to what cereal to eat for breakfast. After all, other kids were watching him, he thought.

Pretty soon, Sean was very popular at camp. He became friends with some of the prettiest girls his age. He started on the camp basketball and baseball teams. He cohosted a show on the radio station once a week with another popular boy. Other campers watched his games and cheered for him. The cheers felt intoxicating to Sean—so did the attention from the girls.

Think About It

- How did Sean get popular? Do you think he was being himself or being who he thought others wanted him to be?

- Why would Sean pay so much attention to what other kids thought about him?

- Why do you think Sean felt so intoxicated by the cheering and attention?

By the end of the second week of summer camp, Sean began to date a popular girl named Lisa. They would hold hands and hang out with other popular kids. Being popular made Sean feel like he was better than other, regular guys. One afternoon, Gabe, who had been his friend the summer before, came up to Sean as he was sitting with Lisa and her friend Izzy on a table in the shade.

"Hey, Sean, wanna come play soccer?" Gabe asked.

Sean looked at Lisa and Izzy, then turned to Gabe. He knew the girls thought Gabe was too geeky to hang out with them.

"Uh, I don't think so. Soccer is for geeks," Sean laughed.

Gabe's whole face turned red. He quickly walked away. Later that afternoon, Sean came up from behind and knocked Gabe to the ground. Gabe was not his only target. Sean pushed a lot of kids around, taunting them and putting them down in front of girls. Doing this made him feel stronger, more powerful—more popular.

Sean figured he had enough friends. He shunned other kids, even though he had things in common with them. If they wanted to play pickup basketball with Sean and his friends, he'd tell them to go away.

Think About It

- Why would Sean feel like he was better than other kids just because he was popular?

- How did popularity change Sean's behavior?

- Why would Sean close his mind to other kids who were potential friends? What do you think will happen because of this?

As the second session began, new kids arrived at camp. A few of them were in Sean's cabin, but he ignored them. He was too cool for them, he thought.

A few of the new kids didn't like the way Sean treated them and other guys. They hated how he would cut in line for the shower and rip on them in

front of girls. Unlike other kids who had tolerated Sean's antics during the first session, these new guys decided to stand up to Sean.

"Hey, dude," Brendan said to Tom one morning, as they cleaned up their bunk. "That Sean kid is such a jerk."

"I know," Tom replied. "He thinks he's all that."

Tom and Brendan came up with a plan to teach Sean a lesson. First, they played simple pranks on Sean. They loosened the screws on his bed so when he got into it, the bed slammed to the floor. They told the girls he was friends with rumors, saying things like he wet the bed and still slept with a blanky.

Two weeks into the second session, Lisa's friend Beth knocked on the door at Sean's cabin. Sean came out to talk to her.

"Hey, Sean," she said. "Lisa asked me to stop by and tell you . . ."

"Where's Lisa?" Sean asked. He nervously looked around, but did not see her anywhere.

"Lisa's not here," Beth said. "But she told me to tell you she's breaking up with you."

Sean was devastated. Lisa wouldn't talk to him anymore. Neither would her friends. Instead, they just laughed at him and gossiped about him. One morning, he was playing basketball when Lisa, Beth, and two other girls walked by. They looked at Sean and giggled. Sean wanted to approach them, but he was too embarrassed.

"What a loser," he heard Lisa say as they walked past the court.

Other boys no longer looked up to Sean.

"Where's Lisa?" Sean asked. He nervously looked around, but did not see her anywhere.

He didn't know what to do. The summer had started off so well . . . but he now realized that being popular had gone to his head. He couldn't wait to get back home and start attending a new school in the fall. At least there he'd have a clean slate.

Think About It

- Did the boys who tricked Sean handle the situation appropriately?
- What else could they have done in the situation?
- Could Sean change the way the kids at camp view him now? If yes, how?

Many middle schoolers want to have a lot of friends. And some don't want just any friends but the "right" ones. At your age, it's only natural to compare yourself to other kids. This is a natural step in your development. You and your peers are trying to establish a social pecking order, even if you don't mean to do it.

While they might seem to be friends with everyone, some popular kids don't have many close friends. Many of them aren't being true to themselves, so people don't even like them for who they really are. Popularity is fleeting. Once they lose their popularity, kids often find that those who they thought were their friends actually hung out with them only for their status.

The desire for popularity may drive boys such as Sean to start acting differently. And that change in behavior can have negative consequences. The need to be popular can turn kids into bullies. So, get the right perspective on popularity. It's better to have a few close friends than a bunch of friends who aren't really true ones.

Work It Out

1. If you find you're not popular at school or camp, figure out what you like to do and join a group of kids your age in that activity. You may find that when you are around other kids who share a similar interest, you'll really be able to act like yourself—no new personality required.

2. Spend more time with family and others who love you. Feeling loved and valued helps guys your age overcome the intense feelings of isolation they experience when being shunned by their peers.

The Last Word from Ryan

Guys your age might think being popular is one of the most important things in their lives. When you get older, you will laugh about how much you worried about popularity as a kid. It's not funny to you now, though. So, check yourself if you find you're suddenly on top of the world: Have humility. Treat other people the way you want to be treated. Do all those things your parents taught you about being respectful. Don't let popularity go to your head and turn you into a jerk. Remember that popularity is fleeting. One day, you may not be so popular. Then, you will want the popular kids to treat you with respect, too.

3
Victim of Bullying

Nobody likes to be picked on or pushed around. But let's face it: It happens to lots of kids. For numerous reasons, some boys become targets for bullies. Maybe they're small or scrawny and can't fend for themselves. Or they're considered dorky or uncool. Perhaps they're just in the wrong place at the wrong time. The point is that being the victim of bullying happens for many reasons, so it can happen to anyone.

Victims of bullying might feel embarrassed, confused, or alienated. They often get so humiliated that they won't tell adults what's going on. Instead, victims simply put up with the bullying, hoping it will somehow just go away.

They feel powerless to stop it and are left feeling helpless and awful.

Amir was a victim of bullying at his middle school. He was going through a weird phase. He suddenly lacked self-confidence and didn't stand up for himself. As a result, Amir became an easy target for bullies. Take a look at Amir's story.

Amir's Story

As an elementary school student, Amir rarely had to deal with bullies. He had plenty of friends and didn't usually have trouble getting along with his classmates—even the difficult ones. When

> Victims of bullying might feel embarrassed, confused, or alienated. They often get so humiliated that they won't tell adults what's going on.

he started middle school, though, Amir suddenly had to deal with a number of changes that made him seem different from other kids. He had to get braces, which made his lower lip stick out. Out of nowhere, he grew a few inches. He became awkward and uncoordinated, which really showed when he tried to play sports. He also had to get glasses. Of course, other boys in Amir's class noticed his change in appearance and his awkwardness.

"Look at that kid," John called out when Amir walked past his locker the morning after he got glasses.

"What a dork," Brad said.

Pedro, Brad, and others made fun of his glasses and braces. They called him names. They laughed at his poor coordination. During gym class one afternoon, Amir fell while trying to grab a rebound. All the boys in class—even some girls—laughed loudly.

But that teasing was nothing compared to what Amir had to deal with from bullies. Some of the bigger, meaner kids in Amir's class often pushed around other kids. So did other kids who had suddenly become popular.

Think About It

- Why would other kids make fun of Amir? Have you ever teased someone because of how he looked?

- Why would kids push each other around? Have you ever bullied other kids?

- Why would some kids start acting like bullies once they've become popular, while other kids might use their popularity to end bullying?

One morning while Amir was waiting for the bus, Evan pulled down Amir's pants. About a dozen kids saw him standing there in his underwear, including a few girls he liked. Jill pointed at him. "Look, tighty whities!" Everyone laughed.

The next week, a couple of bullies cornered Amir in the back of the bus. They pinned him down and gave him a wedgie. Nobody tried to stop them. Other students looked on and cheered. "Wedgieeeeeeee!" they all called out. Amir's face turned bright red. He bit his lip, trying not to cry.

Later, Shoua tripped Amir in the hallway. Another time, Evan pushed him into a locker. Anytime Amir was not paying attention, bullies would punch him in the arm as they walked by.

The bullying made Amir miserable. After a while, he felt like less of a person, like he didn't deserve to be happy. And he didn't know how to make it stop. He didn't want to talk to his parents or teachers about what was going on. He was too humiliated to talk to anyone about it, even his friends.

Then one afternoon in gym class, the bullies ganged up on Amir during a dodge ball game. Shoua threw the ball right at Amir's head so it knocked off his glasses. As he walked out of the gym, Amir tried hard to hold back tears. He could hear the guys laughing as he headed out the door.

Mr. Johnson, Amir's math teacher, was in the hallway and saw him tearing up. "Hey, Amir," Mr. Johnson called to him as he walked down the hall. "Hold up for a second. Are you okay?"

Amir told him, "I'm just having a bad day. I flunked my history test." Talking about the situation with Mr. Johnson was the last thing Amir wanted to do. But Mr. Johnson's concern got Amir thinking about maybe telling his parents sometime.

Think About It

- Why was Amir such a popular target for bullies? Have you ever been a target?
- Why would other kids laugh when Amir was being bullied, instead of helping him?
- Why wouldn't Amir talk to his teacher about the bullying?
- Why does Amir feel like less of a person because of the bullying?

"Amir . . . is everything okay?" Amir's mom put her hand on his forehead as he lay on the couch after school that day.

Amir paused. He wanted to say he was fine, but he couldn't get any words out.

"What's wrong?" his mother asked.

Again, Amir said nothing. He just looked at the floor and tried hard not to cry. This time, though, tears started rolling down his cheeks.

"Tell me what's wrong," his mother begged. "Are you having problems at school?"

"Yes," Amir whispered.

Little by little, Amir told his mother all about the bullying. She was angry. She couldn't believe the school allowed this to go on. "Why didn't you tell me this before?" she demanded. "We need to put a stop to this. This is a serious problem. Your classmates have no right to treat you like this."

The next day, Amir's mother spoke to the principal, Mr. Elliott. He agreed to try to stop the bullying. Mr. Elliott called some of the kids who had been bullying Amir into his office. He sat them across from his desk and looked them in the eye.

"I've been told that some of you have been pushing around one of our students," he said. "This will stop right now."

Mr. Elliott made it clear they were not to bully Amir, or any other kids, anymore.

"If you continue this behavior," he told them, "you will receive detention, suspension, and possibly expulsion."

That afternoon, Amir got on the bus to go home. He felt nervous as he climbed the stairs. No one touched him or called him names, but they watched him. The bullies and their friends shot dirty looks at Amir.

He was relieved to get home. He made it through another day. Amir wasn't sure what the next day would bring, but he no longer felt alone in dealing with the situation.

Think About It

- what do you think prompted Amir to finally tell his mom about the bullying?
- why do you think the principal spoke to Amir's bullies without Amir in the room?
- Do you think the bullying is really over?
- what else could Amir do to help end the bullying?

Bullying is repeated aggression intended to hurt or control another person. It can take the form of physical, verbal, or psychological aggression. It's marked by an imbalance of power between the bully and the victim. According to one study, more than 90 percent of middle school boys have been victims of bullying at least once. Boys are much more likely than girls to be physically bullied.

Being the bullying victim can have dire consequences. Victims of physical bullying are more likely to be sick, see their grades suffer, and feel depressed. Many victims of bullying want to withdraw from other kids, even those who could become friends. Social isolation is not healthy. Just as with Amir, it is important to speak out. Saying something to parents or a trusted adult is the first step in getting help.

Work It Out

1. If you are the victim of bullying, show the bully you have self-confidence and will not waiver. Most bullies want a reaction. Walk away, pretend they are not there, make a joke, buddy up, or speak to them calmly, saying, "I would like you to stop" or "Who are you to make fun of me?"

2. If you cannot get the bully to stop bothering you on your own, privately report the problem to an adult.

3. If you see a kid being bullied, don't just ignore it or join the audience. You'd want someone to help you, so do the same for that person.

The Last Word from Ryan

At some point, most guys deal with bullying. But just because it's common doesn't mean you have to take it. You can learn to deal with bullies. Whatever you do, don't ignore the problem. There's no reason to think or feel that you deserve to be treated cruelly. And, though you may feel afraid or ashamed to reach out for help, don't think twice about it. Dealing with a bully takes courage and strength. The sooner you deal with the problem, the sooner your bully will go away.

4

The Bully

Every place where a group of kids gathers seems to have at least one bully. He messes with other kids for no apparent reason. He pushes kids around or makes fun of them.

Many physical bullies share characteristics. They tend to be aggressive and often have psychological problems. Some have family problems, while others have trouble fitting in with peers. Have you ever considered that you might be a bully? If you are anything like Blake, you might be.

Blake's Story

Blake seemed to be an average kid. He had a younger brother and two

parents who loved him very much. He was athletic, good-looking, and girls talked to him at school. But not everything was easy for Blake. He had a learning disability. Sometimes, it took a long time for something to make sense to him. This held him back in school. If he didn't work hard at his schoolwork every day, he would fall behind.

Blake resented that he had to work harder than other kids just to keep up. When Blake looked at the bright kids, he became even more infuriated. They weren't as athletic or cool as him. Few of them were even popular, which he was. How dare they act like they were better than him.

Blake resented that he had to work harder than they did just to keep up.

Think About It

- Do you have a learning disability? How does it affect learning and studying?

- Why would Blake resent kids he barely knows? What do you think will happen because of his resentment?

Blake eventually started taking out his anger on the kids he resented. Jonah was answering a lot of questions in biology class one afternoon. He was one of the brightest students in the class, with an A average. Blake had just received a D on his last test, even though he'd done all the homework.

This angered Blake. After class, as they walked into the hallway, Blake stuck out his foot and tripped Jonah. "Ooooops," Blake said, laughing.

As he walked away, he heard Jonah whimpering. A few classmates laughed. "Have a nice trip, Jonah?" Ray called out.

For the first time in weeks, Blake felt better about himself. He noticed the same feeling the next day when he made fun of Todd, a bright kid in his history class. Todd wore clothes that were too small for him and parted his hair neatly.

Before class, Blake said to Todd, "You look like a girl with your hair like that. Do you have to get up extra early to make it look so pretty?"

When everyone laughed, Blake felt so good.

With that, the bully was born. Every time Blake felt bad about himself because of his academic problems, he took out his frustration on a classmate. It was always somebody who was smaller than Blake or too unsure socially to talk back to him.

Blake always waited until a group was gathered in a room or on the school bus. He loved to hear his classmates laugh when he bullied other kids.

Think About It

- Why did Blake bully Jonah and Todd? Do you know any bullies like Blake? Do you know any kids like Jonah and Todd who have been bullied?

- Why would Blake bully kids in front of other kids? Why does bullying make him feel good?

- Have you ever acted like Blake? How did you feel?

But not every kid who watched Blake in action laughed. David was a quiet, popular kid who had strong self-esteem. David thought Blake was a jerk for bullying. David couldn't stand to see his classmates humiliated, even those kids he wasn't friends with.

One afternoon, Blake found another target: Brett. He punched Brett in the arm. Then, he grabbed Brett's nipple and twisted it until Brett screamed.

David saw what happened. "Blake, why are you such a bully?" he asked. "You never pick on kids your own size. You never tease anyone who is in the popular crowd. You just pick on people who will give in to you. You think that makes you cool, but it doesn't. It just makes you mean."

Several kids in the group were stunned. "Ooooooh," a few of them said in unison. They figured Blake would attack David next.

But Blake did nothing. He couldn't answer David's questions—at least not out loud. Instead, Blake just walked away, feeling ashamed. He thought about what David had said. He knew he didn't bully stronger kids because he was afraid they would fight back and hurt him. He didn't go after the cool kids because he wanted them to like him. He wanted to stay popular.

After school, Blake ran into Todd on the bus. David and a few kids who had been there before lunch were also there. Remembering how David had shamed him earlier, Blake was eager for attention. He went right for Todd. Blake pushed Todd over and put him in a headlock. He waited for Todd to gasp for air, like he usually did. This time, though, Todd was quiet. When Blake let go, Todd walked away. Todd sat back in his seat and acted like nothing had happened. It seemed that Todd was no longer afraid of Blake. Pretty soon nobody was.

Think About It

- What prompted David to challenge Blake? What do you think the other kids felt and thought when David did so?

- Why didn't Blake retaliate when David challenged him?

- Why do you think Todd was no longer afraid of Blake?

- In bullying situations, which role do you usually play—bully, victim, defender, or bystander?

Bullies enjoy seeing the results of their aggression. They often lack empathy and feelings of guilt. They like to dominate other kids and be in charge and believe that the world owes them something.

Bullies such as Blake are not only physically aggressive. Bullies can also verbally abuse others or use body language to make another person feel uncomfortable, such as rolling their eyes or shaking their heads to destroy another's confidence.

Most bullies are insecure. They try to make up for those insecurities by making other kids uncomfortable. Some bullies are popular kids who thrive on having an audience to witness their bullying. They feel like that makes them more popular. They sometimes prey on kids who are insecure like themselves.

Work It Out

1. Think hard about yourself and your social interactions with others. Do you resent others? Do you enjoy seeing other people in pain or discomfort? Do you lash out at others to hide an insecurity of your own? Consider the fact that continuing these actions could be thought of as bullying.

2. If you are a bully, volunteer work should help you develop empathy for others.

3. If frustration with a personal problem is causing you to bully, address that problem. Talk to a parent or another adult about your behavior. Ask them for tips for coping with your anger.

4. Apologize to kids you have harmed.

5. If you see bullying, step in to stop it.

The Last Word from Ryan

Bullying has become a common problem in schools. The National Center for Education Statistics reports that there's more bullying in middle schools than in high schools. Being a bully does not just mean pushing kids around or doling out wedgies. You can be a bully with your words and body language, too. Sometimes, you are bullying kids without even meaning to. Guys your age are constantly trying to find their roles in the world and asserting dominance over each other. It's a natural part of growing up. Sometimes, you get carried away and may bully another kid. That's when you need to pull yourself back in. Think about what it's like to be the bully's victim. You can assert yourself without being so nasty. Be subtle and understanding. These attributes are a big part of adult life.

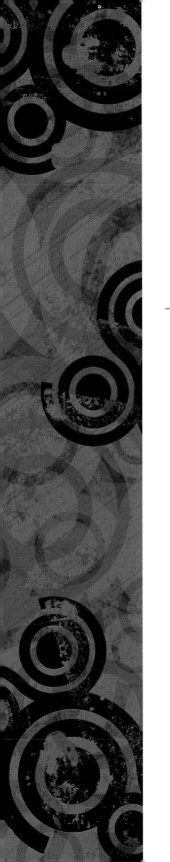

5

Class Clown

Paying attention in class can be hard sometimes. You have to sit still and focus on a subject that may not interest you. That can drive some guys to act out. They may make faces, crack jokes, or make noises. They do whatever they can for attention. You probably know at least one of these guys. He is the class clown.

Being a class clown can be fun. To an extent, you get away with acting out. Classmates laugh at your jokes, which can make you feel popular. You don't have to take school so seriously.

But being the class clown usually doesn't work out in the long run. Everybody is in school for a reason: to

learn and to prepare for adulthood. When you're clowning around, you often aren't learning. You may also be distracting and making it hard for others to learn. That was the case for Aaron.

Aaron's Story

Aaron was a good student in his middle school. He loved his math and history classes, especially. Hebrew school, which he attended as a Jewish youth, was a different story.

Being a class clown can be fun. To an extent, you get away with acting out.

Twice a week after school, Aaron had to attend Hebrew school for two hours. He thought Hebrew school was not as important as regular school. His parents rarely asked

him if he had done his Hebrew schoolwork. They never asked him about his Hebrew school grades. But they always wanted to see his report card from middle school. They also allowed him to skip Hebrew school to practice baseball and basketball.

Aaron usually behaved in regular school. But he often acted up in Hebrew school.

In Aaron's Hebrew school class, he acted out so much that one day his teacher, Ms. Schwartz, scowled at him. "Aaron," she said, "your behavior is not acceptable. You are acting like a class clown."

Much of the class laughed. So did Aaron. He took the label as an honor. During class, he loudly chewed gum. He played paper football in the back of the room with a classmate. He stood on his chair and stretched, hoping his classmates would notice and laugh. He whispered jokes to kids sitting next to him. When Ms. Schwartz called on him, he gave foolish answers.

"Aaron, who led the Israelites out of Egypt in Exodus?" she asked one afternoon.

"I don't know," he replied. "Brett Favre?"

All the boys in class laughed. So did a few of the girls. They also laughed at the noises he sometimes made: fart noises with his armpits and clicking noises with his tongue.

Think About It

- Why didn't Aaron take Hebrew school as seriously as regular school? Why would Aaron act out so much in Hebrew school class? Have you ever acted like Aaron in a classroom?

- Why would Aaron consider it an honor to be named class clown? Do you have a class clown at your school? Is he or she funny all the time or annoying?

All of this behavior annoyed Aaron's teacher. Aaron made it hard for her to focus on her lesson plan. He also annoyed classmates who wanted to

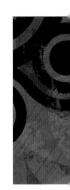

learn. Many of the girls in his class especially disliked him. "You are sooo immature," Brittany said to him one afternoon.

But that only made Aaron try harder to make her laugh.

After a few weeks, Aaron's mother attended a back-to-school night at his Hebrew school.

"Mrs. Silver, I want to talk to you about your son, Aaron," Ms. Schwartz said.

"Is something wrong?" Aaron's mother asked.

"He is out of control and has no respect for this class," she promptly responded.

Something had to be done, they agreed. "I'm not sure Aaron is being challenged in this class," Aaron's mother told Ms. Schwartz. "It may move too slowly for him." Mrs. Silver noted that Aaron's grades were not bad and he usually did well on tests. So, she knew that even though he was acting like a clown, he had no trouble learning the material. "Why don't we move him to another class?" Mrs. Silver suggested. "Not just any class, but the advanced class."

Think About It

- Do you think Aaron cared about how his behavior impacted other students?

- Why would Aaron's mother suggest moving him to the advanced class? What do you think will happen there?

- Has a teacher or parent ever moved you to a different class? Why?

At the end of the quarter, Aaron was moved to the advanced class. At first, he tried to be a clown. He made the usual noises and faces, cracked jokes, and blew bubbles with his gum.

But Aaron's classmates didn't seem to notice. One afternoon, Aaron blew a large bubble and let it burst, sticking to his face. He waited for laughter, but none came. Instead, his classmates paid attention to their teacher. Their class was much more difficult than Aaron's previous class had been. They had to focus to keep up and get the grades they wanted. Many of them were excellent students who didn't care to joke around.

But Aaron still wanted to clown around. The next day, he came to class dressed in the superhero costume he had worn for Halloween the previous year. He was sure everyone would laugh when he walked through the door.

But no one did. Some of the kids rolled their eyes, others just looked at him briefly. They all just focused on their studies. Aaron couldn't believe it. Were they just ignoring him? After class that day,

Mark leaned over and said, "Nice costume, but Halloween is still a month away."

Aaron didn't know what to say.

Mark went on, "Look, you're a funny guy, but you're really distracting. How do you get good grades when you never pay attention in class?"

Aaron was stunned. He hadn't heard such honest words from another guy in his class before. The whole walk home, Aaron thought about what Mark had said.

Aaron was stunned. He hadn't heard such honest words from another guy in his class before.

Think About It

- why would Aaron's new classmates ignore his behavior? what do you think Aaron thought when he couldn't get a reaction out of them?

- How did changing classes affect Aaron?

- why do you think Mark said what he did? why was his opinion so surprising to Aaron?

Almost every class has a kid like Aaron. The class clown can be a huge distraction to the rest of the class, and to himself. These kids act like clowns for numerous reasons. Perhaps they are bored by the class, not challenged by the material, can't sit still, or desperately need attention.

Class clowns like Aaron can easily be addressed. When a kid is not being challenged by his class, moving him to a more advanced class might work. But other class clowns have more severe conditions. Some class clowns act out for attention or adoration from their peers. They may be compensating for problems they have at home. Some may be diagnosed with ADHD and have trouble concentrating in class. Others have learning problems or are socially insecure and act out to compensate for those issues. They hope their peers don't notice their problems. But they do.

Work It Out

1. If classmates or teachers call you a class clown, think about why you are acting out. Do you need attention? Are you bored with your schoolwork? Would you benefit from harder material?

2. Whether you can determine the reason for your clowning or not, ask an adult for help. Being a clown only holds you back. It also harms classmates by distracting them from the lesson. It may seem fun, but you need to put a stop to it.

3. If you feel the need to act out and be dramatic, find an outlet for that behavior. Take an acting class, try out for a school play, or join a community theater group.

4. Get involved in sports or another lively activity like martial arts. This will help you burn energy and make it easier to pay attention in class.

The Last Word from Ryan

Some of the best comedians on TV will say that they were class clowns in school. But even these successful guys will say they regret missing out on learning stuff. If you can make people laugh, you definitely have a gift. You don't have to squelch it. But there's a time and a place for everything. Besides, the best comics need material to work from. Pay attention in school, and you'll learn some great stuff for your act.

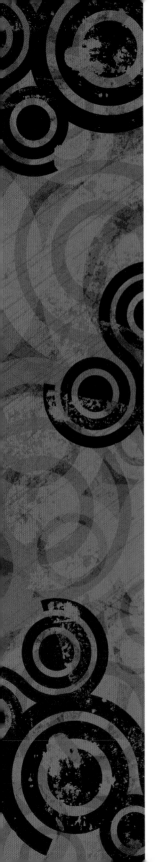

6

Trying on Labels

I t started with toys and cereal. Now, it's apparel and sneakers. Pretty soon, it may be cars and gadgets. Throughout your life, you will be bombarded with advertisements from people trying to get you to buy stuff. Some of them are hard to resist.

It's especially difficult as an adolescent. Because you are still figuring out who you are, you may be on the lookout for the next hot product to identify with. Look around your school. You probably see kids exhibiting any number of styles. Many of them will change by this time next year.

Some kids go overboard. In an attempt to fit in or find an identity, they jump from one fad to the next. Many of these fads don't fit them at all, but they are desperate to try them out. These guys seem oblivious to how silly they may look.

Kevin was a kid who always wanted to be ahead of the curve with new styles and trends. He thought they would make him more popular and make classmates think he was cool. But he learned he was wrong.

Kevin's Story

When he started middle school, Kevin suddenly started to pay a lot of attention to his appearance—especially what he wore. He noticed that many of the eighth

Kevin was a kid who always wanted to be ahead of the curve with new styles and trends. He thought they would make him more popular and make classmates think he was cool.

graders looked much cooler than he did. They seemed to be popular, talked to girls, and looked happy. *I want to be like that,* Kevin thought.

Of course he couldn't be *exactly* like the other kids, so he settled for what he considered the next-best thing: to act and look just like the most popular kids in school. Not many of Kevin's friends followed the trends, but Kevin decided he would have to be stylish if he wanted to be popular.

At the time, all kinds of fads had infiltrated Kevin's school. Many guys wore baggy, dark jeans

like their older brothers in high school. The middle school kids wore fitted hats with straight bills. They tilted the hats sideways, just like star professional and college athletes. They talked like the hip-hop artists they saw in music videos. The kids used slang and terms rappers used, even though most of them didn't know what the terms meant.

Think About It

- why do you think many boys in Kevin's school followed the popular trends they saw older boys and men exhibiting?

- why did Kevin want to be like them?

- Have you ever adopted a fad or followed a trend? what happened?

Kevin adopted all those fads. After all, he wanted to look like he fit in. By the end of his first semester of middle school, his friends didn't recognize him anymore. Kevin had been a quiet, studious kid who wore whatever T-shirts and track pants his mom bought for him. He had always been polite. He used to listen to songs by the Beatles and Bruce Springsteen that his parents played at home.

Now, Kevin wore black hats that still had the labels on the brim. He turned them sideways. He

watched hip-hop videos over and over again on his computer. He memorized some of the lines and repeated them out loud at school. He started wearing his baggy jeans pulled down low, showing his boxer shorts. When he spoke to his parents, Kevin repeated the slang terms he heard in the videos and had seen in his new favorite television shows.

"What's up with Kevin?" Brandon said to Billy one morning at the bus stop.

Kevin adopted all those fads. After all, he wanted to look like he fit in. By the end of his first semester of middle school, his friends didn't recognize him anymore.

"I know," Billy said. "He's gotten weird."

Kevin's parents only shook their heads and tried to ignore his behavior.

"He's going through a phase," his mother said.

"How long is this phase going to last?" his father shot back. "He's getting to be obnoxious."

Think About It

- what do Kevin's parents mean when they say he's going through a phase?

- Have you ever changed your entire appearance and tastes so much that your friends didn't recognize you? why did you do it?

- why do you think Kevin changed so much, so quickly?

One day after school, Kevin's old friend Nate called to him across the hallway. "Kevin! Will you sit by me on the bus? I've got some new songs we can listen to on my iPod," Nate yelled.

Kevin was embarrassed. He was walking with a group of his new friends—the guys who dressed like him—and he didn't want to be seen hanging out with Nate. Kevin turned his shoulder and pretended he hadn't heard Nate. He knew it was wrong, but he

didn't care. He had more important people to hang out with.

By the end of the school year, Kevin had completely stopped hanging out with many of his old friends. His new friends were into the same styles he

was, but Kevin had trouble connecting with them. Kevin wanted to play basketball with them just as he had with his old friends. But few of them liked the game. He wanted to play for them a Beatles song he really liked, but they didn't want to hear it.

Think About It

- Why would Kevin abandon his old friends?

- Have you ever mistreated an old friend because you were trying to impress a new one? What happened?

- What do you think will happen with Kevin and his new group of friends?

Kevin was confused. If his new friends seemed to be so much like him on the outside, why couldn't he connect with them? Also, Kevin started to think about his summer. The past summer, he and Nate had spent time together shooting hoops and listening to their favorite music. If his new friends didn't enjoy the same activities, what would he do all summer? Who would he hang out with? Who would he shoot hoops with? Kevin sat in his room, alone. He put in his earbuds and turned on his favorite Beatles song. He pulled out his cell phone and looked at his contact list. Nate was still at the top of it.

Think About It

- Why did Kevin find it hard to connect with his new friends?

- What did Kevin realize about his friendship with Nate?

- Do you think Nate will forgive Kevin? Why or why not?

As you get older, you might feel as if fitting in with the popular crowd is a high priority. This can involve having the right clothes, saying the right things, and even ditching your old friends. Finding your identity is important. Unfortunately, it can lead to disastrous results if you don't understand that friendship is more than fashion. Solid friendships involve trust, respect, and communication.

Remember that changing yourself to fit in might change your group of friends, too. Like Kevin, you might realize that your new friends are nothing like you. You might dress the same, but the similarities could end there. So, before you ditch your old group to fit in with a new one, think about the friends who stuck by you before you started looking cool. Chances are they like you for who you really are—not for how you look.

Work It Out

1. It's okay to follow new styles, but try to mix them with your own personality and style. Wear the trendy new hat with the same shirts you always wear. Wear styles that make you feel like you and that feel comfortable.

2. Understand that fads constantly change.

3. If you find yourself tempted to change your appearance to fit in with a new group, stop and consider the fact that friendship is more than clothes. Do you want friends who like you because of how you dress or because of who you are? Plus, keeping up with the latest styles quickly adds up. Wearing the hottest new clothes is expensive.

The Last Word from Ryan

Celebrities and models can look cool sporting new gear and new styles, and these styles eventually make their way to schools. It's hard to resist copying their looks—after all, it's human nature to want to fit in and be accepted. Try to resist fitting in if it requires a radical change in who you choose to hang out with. As you figure out your identity, don't put up a false front. Adopt styles that work best for you. Does a style feel natural? If not, drop it. You may think you look cool by following a new style. But if you are trying on a label that does not fit you, you may actually look ridiculous, and you may alienate your old friends. Stay true to yourself.

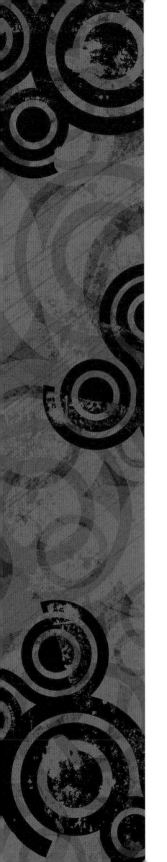

7

Leaving Friends Behind

L eaving friends behind is one of the most difficult things some guys have to do. Suddenly, your family moves to a new town or you transfer to a different school. You were used to seeing your friends almost every day. Now, you see them once a week, once a month, or only once a year.

When a guy moves, he loses the daily support of old friends whom he trusted. Suddenly, he's surrounded by kids he barely knows. And no parent, teacher, or coach can fill the void—no matter how hard they try.

Ron is one guy who had this experience when he moved to a new school. He started sixth grade in one

school, while most of his friends enrolled at another. Take a look at Ron's story to see how he coped with the anxiety of leaving friends behind.

Ron's Story

Ron had been happy at his elementary school. It was close to home, so he walked there every morning with his little brother and his friends Steve and John. Ron would spend recess playing football or basketball with his friends. After school, he competed on organized sports teams with those same friends. He volunteered at the school store and knew many of the teachers.

> When a guy moves, he loses the daily support of old friends whom he trusted. Suddenly, he's surrounded by kids he barely knows.

After fifth grade, Ron's parents transferred him to a private school. They said the new school would "challenge him more academically" and "provide more structure."

"This will help you become a better student and learn discipline," his father said.

"Do I have to?" Ron asked.

"Yes, you do."

Think About It

- Why was Ron so comfortable at his elementary school?

- Are you happy with your group of friends? What would you do if you had to leave them behind?

Ron's father was right about the new school. Ron's sixth grade classes were much harder than his classes had been at the old school, and his teachers expected him to be more organized and more respectful in class. But moving to a new school had negative consequences, too. For the first time he could remember, Ron was not around his friends every day. In fact, he barely saw them at all.

Ron missed his old friends. Most of them still attended school together. They hung out all the time and made more friends at their middle school. With the longer drive home from school, Ron missed a lot of fun every afternoon. Ron worried that he would be abandoned by his old buddies because he was suddenly not at school with them.

"Mom," he said to his mother one night shortly after school started in the fall, "what if my old friends don't want to hang out with me anymore?"

"They're all in the neighborhood. You'll still see them around," his mother replied, but Ron didn't feel any better. He just wasn't sure.

Think About It

- Why did Ron feel isolated without his old friends around?

- Have you ever moved away from close friends? Were you able to keep in touch with them?

- Why was Ron so anxious about what his old friends were up to?

In winter, basketball season started and Ron rejoined a few of his friends on their league team. His face broke into a broad smile when he saw Ross, David, and a few other old friends on the first day of practice. He hadn't smiled so big in a while. "Hey guys," he called out as he walked into the gym. The other boys looked at Ron and smiled. "Dude," David said, "where have you been?"

At first, Ron felt like nothing had changed. But he realized that he was left out of a lot of conversations. When the guys talked about the time Mr. Wallace's toupee fell off in class, Ron thought the story was funny—but he hadn't been there to see it. And they had all kinds of inside jokes that Ron didn't get. He couldn't figure out why they all yelled out "Kidneys!" and laughed hysterically when someone did something stupid—but he didn't want to ask, either.

Ron was sad that he was growing apart from his old friends. But he really liked some of the new friends he was making, like Barry from his science class. He wondered if maybe moving on was for the best.

Think About It

- Have you ever reunited with old friends after being apart for a long time? How did that feel?

- Do you agree with Ron that moving on to new friends is "for the best"?

Friends are invaluable. Your parents make a lot of decisions for you, such as where to live and go to school, what to eat, and even what clothes to wear. But who you make friends with is mainly up to you. Friends provide support and validation—the acceptance and understanding all kids need from their peers. Friendships help you understand your place in the world. Friends help you feel connected and not so alone. Sometimes, we change or move on while our friends go in a different direction. But don't give up too easily—the oldest friends can be the truest, even if you can't see each other every day. And new friends, if you keep an open mind, can be the beginning of some exciting experiences.

Work It Out

1. If moving or changing schools separates you from friends, the friendship doesn't have to end. Recognize that although you might not have the same experiences anymore, you can still be friends.

2. If you feel left out of an inside joke, you may have to accept that some things are not what they used to be. Focus on the experiences you still share and making new memories instead.

3. If you have a group of "old friends" and a different group of "new friends," see what happens if you get them all together at the same time. Try setting up a baseball game or inviting everyone to see a movie together. Maybe you can help the two groups become one.

The Last Word from Ryan

Almost every kid has to go through a separation from friends, whether it's you or your friend moving away. That does not make it any easier to deal with. A friendship is a relationship. So, growing apart from a friend can be an emotional experience. Don't let this experience get you down for too long. Try to make new friends. And keep in touch with your old friends. You never know if you might run into each other again.

8

The New Kid

Some kids end up being the new guy at school—sometimes, repeatedly. That can make for an uncomfortable experience. They don't know any classmates. Other kids ignore them. Sometimes, kids treat them badly because they are new and different.

It can be hard for the new guy to fit in and concentrate on his studies. He may feel so down that he does not want to join any clubs or sports teams after school. Dan was once a new kid like that.

Dan's Story

Dan was a gangly, awkward kid. He was not a great athlete or a good student,

either. He had trouble paying attention. But Dan had done okay in school because he worked hard at it. He felt comfortable at his Pennsylvania middle school and with his small circle of friends.

That changed when Dan's family moved to Washington DC right after winter break. Dan had to start at a new school in the middle of the school year. He walked into homeroom one early January morning, sat down, and was met by about two dozen faces he didn't recognize. He sunk into his seat and ducked his head low. He hoped nobody would notice him.

It can be hard for the new guy to fit in and concentrate on his studies. He may feel so down that he does not want to join any clubs or sports teams after school.

That worked for a few minutes. Then, roll call started. "Daniel Simpson," Ms. Claiborne called out.

"Here," he responded meekly.

The other students were surprised to hear a new name, and several turned around when Dan spoke.

"Class, we have a new student with us this morning," Ms. Claiborne said. "Daniel just moved here from Pennsylvania. Please welcome him. Daniel, introduce yourself."

Dan stood up. His voice quivered, and his body shook a bit. "Uh, my name is Daniel Simpson," he said. "I grew up in York, in Pennsylvania. I moved here last week."

Think About It

- why would Dan try to avoid being noticed by his new classmates?

- why do you think Dan was so nervous about introducing himself? Have you ever been nervous about meeting new kids?

At lunch and recess, Dan's new classmates surrounded him.

"What's Pennsylvania like?" Chris wondered.

"Why did you move here?" Kelsey asked.

"Uh, I moved here because my dad got a new job," Dan replied. "Pennsylvania is okay, I guess."

"So do you, like, play baseball or anything?" Chris went on.

"What kind of music do you listen to?" Kelsey asked. "I love hip-hop."

"No, I don't really like baseball, but I like basketball. No, I don't listen to hip-hop." Dan liked the interest the kids showed in him, but he felt so different from them. He didn't seem to like what they liked. *I'm never going to fit in*, he thought to himself. He just wanted the school day to end.

Dan sat through a few more classes and was barraged by more questions until the day finally ended. He trudged home from the bus stop and walked in the front door.

"How was your first day?" His mom asked cheerfully. "Did you make any new friends?"

"Mom, do I have to go back tomorrow?" he asked, though he knew what her answer would be.

His mother chuckled. "Of course you do, honey. But cheer up. It'll get better. Just be yourself."

Think About It

- why do you think Dan wanted the other kids in class to leave him alone?

- why would Dan want to stay away from school? Have you ever wanted to avoid a place because you were new?

Dan didn't feel encouraged by his mom's words. He went to bed dreading going to school the next day. The rest of the week was just as tough for Dan. The kids kept asking him questions, and Dan felt like he kept giving the wrong answers. He got less and less talkative as the week went on. Soon, the others stopped talking to him all together.

Dan didn't know what to do to fit in better. He couldn't pretend to like things he wasn't interested in. The kids in his classes had learned to ignore him because he wouldn't carry on a conversation with them. Dan was miserable. His grades were starting to suffer because he wouldn't speak in class and did poorly on group projects.

Dan got into the habit of eating his lunch really fast and then going to the library to read by himself for the rest of the period. One day, he had just settled in at one of the tables to start his favorite author's new graphic novel, when he heard the chair across from him moving. A guy who he'd seen in the hall but never met sat down across from him.

"Hi," the other guy said. "I'm Steve. You're Dan, right? You moved here a few weeks ago?"

"Yeah," said Dan, warily. "From Pennsylvania."

"He's my favorite author," said Steve, pointing to Dan's book. "I haven't read the new one yet."

"He's great, right?" replied Dan, warming up. "You wanna borrow it when I'm done?"

The guys talked about graphic novels until lunch was over. Dan went to his next class with a new spring in his step. *Maybe there is someone in this school I can talk to*, he thought.

Think About It

- Why did Dan have so much trouble fitting in with his new classmates?

- Why did Dan start to struggle with schoolwork? Has a personal problem ever affected your schoolwork?

- Why did one conversation make such a difference to Dan? Do you think he will start making more friends now?

Ask Dr. Robyn

Being the new kid can be challenging. You don't know the kids around you, so you don't know how they will react to you. You may fear they don't like you, even though they don't know you yet. Everything, from the classrooms to the people in charge, seems foreign.

Whenever you start something new in new surroundings, you have to make numerous personal adjustments. You have to adapt to the rules and expectations of the adults in charge. You have to start over in developing relationships with people around you. To complicate matters, most of the other kids know each other.

Remember, though, that most kids are open to making new friends. Don't give up on making friends if you are the new kid. Give people a chance, and they will likely give you a chance, too.

Work It Out

1. Join extracurricular activities such as sports teams, band, or theater groups. This will help you meet kids who have similar interests.

2. Don't judge your new classmates. Keep an open mind about them, even if they don't have an open mind about you. Give them time to start opening up to you. Be prepared when they finally do. Ask good questions to show you are interested in getting to know them, and listen patiently to the answers. Being a good listener can go a long way.

3. Focus on your studies and other activities you can control. Making new friends will come in time. Focusing your mind on something else will help you stay calm until you get to know other kids better.

The Last Word from Ryan

I remember the fear and anxiety of being the new kid. I was not alone. Only the most extroverted guys enjoy being the new kid. Most of us hate it. Even so, you need to overcome the terror that guys in Dan's situation experience. Think of being the new kid as an opportunity to make new friends and learn more about yourself. You can be whomever you want. You are not trapped by the role you had with your old friends. Being thrust into a classroom full of kids you don't know could be just the spark you need.

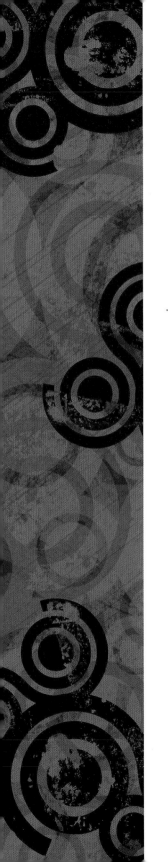

9

Cultural Differences

Sometimes, cultural differences can make it hard to fit in. Imagine moving to the United States from another country. Even if you were born in the United States, your family still might follow many of the same traditions they did in the country they moved from. These differences can definitely make a kid stand out.

Life can be complicated for a guy with cultural differences. While many of his classmates eat pizza and play football, he may eat shepherd's pie, a traditional English food, and love soccer. As a result, he might not click with many classmates or have a lot of friends. He is eager to fit in, but it might be difficult.

Raphael struggled to overcome cultural differences with his classmates. His family moved from Brazil to the United States. Raphael barely spoke English and knew nothing about U.S. culture, except for what he saw in the movies and on television. Take a look at Raphael's story to see how he handled this situation.

Raphael's Story

Raphael came from a large Brazilian family. He grew up playing soccer with his brothers and going to the beach near his family's house. He was competitive and smart, and lots of guys wanted to be his friend.

Life can be complicated for a guy with cultural differences. While many of his classmates eat pizza and play football, he may eat shepherd's pie, a traditional English food, and love soccer.

When Raphael was 12, his family moved to the United States. Raphael quickly realized that his new classmates were different from his friends in Brazil. On his first day of school, many of them organized a football game at recess. Raphael joined in.

But he was surprised when they started throwing around a funny-shaped brown ball with white stripes. "Football?" he wondered out loud. "This is football?"

"Yeah," Michael answered. "What did you think we were going to do?"

HURON PUBLIC LIBRARY
521 DAKOTA AVE S
HURON, SD 57350

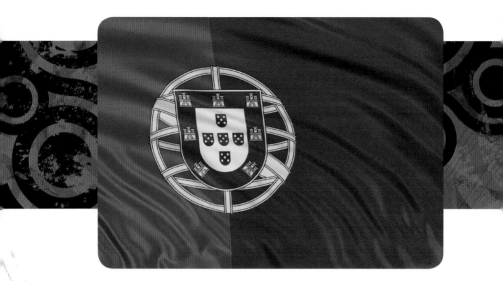

Raphael had expected them to be kicking around a soccer ball. In Brazil, kids called soccer *futbol*, which sounds like "football."

Raphael's new classmates were different in other ways, too. They only went to the beach during the summer, because it was a few hours away. Worst of all, none of them spoke a word of Portuguese. That was the only language Raphael knew well.

Raphael was determined to fit in at his new school. At first, that was difficult. Raphael joined the football games his classmates played during recess. But he didn't know the rules of American football. One morning, he tackled a classmate after the boy had stepped out of bounds. Raphael did not understand the play had ended.

"Raphael!" Michael yelled. "What the heck are you doing?"

On another play, he tried to kick the ball instead of throw it. "Raphael," Justin said, sounding agitated, "we're not attempting a field goal now."

Football has so many weird rules, Raphael thought.

Think About It

- Describe a situation where everyone was different from you. How did you handle it?

- Is there anyone in your class from another culture? How are you different? How are you alike?

- Would being different from your classmates make you feel uneasy or uncertain about yourself?

Most of the time, Raphael could barely understand what his classmates were saying. When he started his new school, he was placed in a special class with other students who primarily spoke languages other than English.

One day in the cafeteria, a popular kid named Scott called Raphael over to his table. Raphael felt special that Scott had singled him out. "Hey, Raphael," Scott said, "sit down. We were just talking about that new spy movie that came out this weekend. Did you see it?"

"No," Raphael answered. He was embarrassed. He had no idea what Scott was talking about, but the other guys seemed to be excited about the movie.

"I loved that chase scene," Scott continued. "Remember what the spy called the bad guys?" The other guys laughed and said the word aloud. It was a new word to Raphael.

"Yeah," piped in Jack. "That actor's so cool. You should really see that movie, Raphael."

Raphael knew he probably wouldn't even understand the movie if he saw it. But he remembered the word the guys had said. If that movie was so cool, then that word must be cool, too.

It wasn't until later, when a teacher overheard him saying the word in the hallway, that he learned it wasn't so cool after all. He was so embarrassed when he found out what the word meant.

Think About It

- what do you think it would be like to move to a place where everyone spoke a different language?
- Do you think the boys tricked Raphael into saying a bad word? why or why not?

Raphael was upset about what had happened. He told his mom about it when he got home.

"Mom," he said in Portuguese, "I had no idea what that word meant. If I had, I wouldn't have said it."

"Raphael, you can't let it get you down," his mom said as she brought him a glass of guava juice. "I know you are trying hard to fit in. I'm really proud of you. As for the prank—well, now you've learned your lesson. You are kind of vulnerable as the new kid. Plus, you are still learning the language. Just take it slowly. You'll get there."

"But Mom, what should I do? I want to fit in, but I don't want to play football all the time. I want to play soccer, like I did in Brazil."

"So, why don't you, honey? Let's sign you up for a team. That way, you'll meet boys who like soccer just as much as you do. And as for the language, well, your father and I want you and your brothers to sign up for extra English classes on Saturday mornings. We think they will help a lot."

Raphael agreed. He was excited about the soccer league. As much as he wanted to fit in with his new classmates, he didn't want to forget everything about his Brazilian culture. It was an important part of who he was.

Think About It

- Have you ever taken interest in a new culture? Was it difficult to understand?

- Do you think joining a soccer team and taking English classes will help Raphael be more comfortable with U.S. culture? Why or why not?

Raphael's English improved quickly. Now, he could understand what his classmates were saying. He was able to move out of the special education class he started in to the larger class that was conducted fully in English.

Raphael loved his soccer league. He discovered that, although most of his classmates preferred football, plenty of American kids also liked soccer. And Raphael was great at soccer. He was instantly one of the top players on his team. He scored a ton of goals playing forward.

At the end of the season, Raphael's teammates were invited to his house for a party. His mother cooked them an authentic Brazilian lunch.

"Wow, what is this?" Zach asked as he dug into a second helping.

"Fried plantains," Raphael replied, in perfect English.

"It's really good," Zach said.

Zach also found it fascinating when Raphael and his mother spoke to each other in Portuguese. "Hey, Raphael," Zach said, "could you teach me some Portuguese?"

"*Sim*," Raphael replied in Portuguese. "Sure."

Think About It

- How did Raphael overcome his cultural differences?

- Why do you think Raphael invited his teammates to his house for a party at the end of the soccer season?

- Have you ever gone to the house of a friend from another culture?

Kids are naturally curious. Yet, many become suspicious and hesitant around different or unfamiliar things, including people. It's important to be open to different kinds of kids and learn to accept those, like Raphael, who come from other cultures. Throughout your life, you will have the opportunity to work with and be around people from cultures other than your own.

Culture has a great impact on people. It influences their thoughts, actions, relationships, worldviews, and goals. When you embrace people from other cultures, it helps you understand the world better and can make for valuable friendships.

If your family is culturally different from other families in your area, don't be embarrassed or try to hide who you are. While you may not share all the same interests as your new friends, that doesn't mean your interests are wrong or weird. Be open to learning about the new culture around you, but also allow your friends to get to know about your culture. You may find they are just as curious and interested about you as you are about them. And remember, the United States is made up of people from all different cultures.

Work It Out

1. Talk to your relatives about your culture. Ask them about your family origins and what your traditions are. Once you understand where you come from, you can better appreciate people from other cultures.

2. Seek out kids from other cultures. Talk about your own culture with them. Have them talk to you about their culture. They will help you to understand your own better.

3. Watch documentaries and nonfiction movies. Read books that take place in other parts of the world. These things will help you understand those other cultures even more.

The Last Word from Ryan

At your age, the differences can make you feel uncomfortable. Just when you think you've started to figure out the world, you realize there's still so much you don't know. You don't need to feel intimidated by somebody from another culture. Treat meeting him or her as a learning opportunity. The more you learn about different cultures, the more aware and cultured you'll become. This will help you learn about and deal with people in the future.

10
The Gang

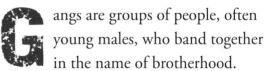

Gangs are groups of people, often young males, who band together in the name of brotherhood. Yet, they can be violent and sometimes engage in illegal behavior such as drug dealing, theft, and assault. Gangs might fight with other gangs or other groups of people. Many gang members often end up in jail—or worse.

Guys might join gangs to feel secure and popular. You might feel that joining a gang will help you stay safe. It may be tempting to join a gang if your family isn't involved in your life or if you wish you had more friends. Maybe you live in a poorer part of the city or you're not doing well in school, and you

think this will be a way to make you feel better about yourself. But gangs are dangerous and can lead you down the wrong path.

In some neighborhoods, though, it seems like everyone is in a gang—maybe even someone in your own family. You may feel pressure to go into the family "business." Or maybe you live in a part of the city that has so many gangs it could

> Guys might join gangs to feel secure and popular. You might feel that joining a gang will help you stay safe.

be dangerous if you didn't join one. If a guy grows up in an area with a lot of gang activity, he may not even think joining a gang is a choice. Michael found himself in this situation.

Michael's Story

"Bye, Michael, have a good day," Tina said as she climbed into the bus.

"Bye, Tina. See you later," he said.

Each day before he walked to school, Michael stayed at the bus stop with his little sister, Tina, to make sure she got safely on the bus. Their mom worked two jobs, and she was already at her first one before Michael or Tina woke up in the morning. Michael would never let his sister wait alone outside their apartment, so he had to wait with her.

Michael and his family lived in a large, busy city. The area was pretty run-down, and it had more than its share of gang activity. Gun shots and police or ambulance sirens could often be heard at night. Michael's mom often shut their apartment windows to drown out the sound.

Think About It

- why do you think Michael has to wait with his sister? what do you think could happen if he didn't?

- what do you think goes through Michael's mind when he hears the sirens each night? why do you think his mom tries to drown out their sound?

As Michael walked to school that morning, he thought about his neighborhood and his initiation

that night. He had to use two hands to count the number of times he'd been approached by gang members. Although he tried to keep his cool, each time they talked to him he felt a sinking feeling in his gut and his heartbeat raced. The threats to him and his sister were getting to be too much. He saw what happened to guys who didn't join up. It wasn't pretty.

In the hallway at school, Michael ran into Sam.

"You ready for tonight?" Sam asked him.

"Yeah, man, I'm ready. I'll see you at 10. You still can't tell me what's going on?" Michael asked.

"No, you'll find out soon enough."

As Michael walked into class, he thought about Sam's last comment. Why did he need to wear all black? To rob someplace? He didn't think that'd be that bad. He knew initiations could be much worse. Sam was initiated last month by being beaten. He almost had to go to the hospital, and the last of his cuts and bruises were still noticeable.

Think About It

- Why is Michael joining a gang? What would you do in his situation?

- Why can't Michael just ignore the gang members and do his own thing? Do you think he's thought about that? If so, what do you think his conclusion was?

- Have you ever known someone who joined a gang? Why do you think he joined?

At 10:00 o'clock that night, Michael met some of the members of Sam's gang in an abandoned parking lot. His palms were sweating as he walked up to them.

Croz, one of the leaders, spoke first. He told Michael the gang's initiations were meant to weed out the guys who weren't tough enough to make it in. Each member protected the others, and they had to be sure he was willing to do anything for them.

"Do you know what 'blood in, blood out' is?" the leader asked.

"I've heard of it," Michael said.

"Well, it's pretty simple. To get in, blood's gotta spill. Either your own or someone else's. You're lucky, cuz tonight it's someone else's."

He told Michael that a rival gang was encroaching on their territory, and that they needed to be taught a lesson. Michael was the one who would do it. His initiation was to stab one of the rival gang's members.

"You ready?" the gang leader asked.

If Michael did this, he'd be in. He'd have protection for himself and his sister. But would he get caught? What would happen then? And he had to stab this guy. He might kill him. But if he didn't stab the guy, Sam's gang would beat him badly—he'd heard the stories—and probably be out for him in the future. He'd be unprotected.

Michael hesitated, and then he answered.

Think About It

- What do you think Michael's answer will be? If you were in his position, what would you do?

- Can Michael get out of this situation without joining the gang? If so, how? Do you think he'd have to worry about his safety afterward?

- Have you ever been in a situation like Michael's? Have you ever had to make a hard decision that could end negatively either way? How did you decide?

Gang activity is most popular among high school students. This is especially true in low-income areas. There, many boys are pressured by peers to join gangs, and some feel they have to join a gang for safety. They consider joining a gang their only option in life.

Territoriality often breeds gangs. Guys relate to a specific area as their home, as well as the home of their family and friends. They want to protect that territory at all costs. So, they form a gang. When a rival gang invades their territory, violence can result. Many gang members deal drugs. They might make some money from this and other illegal activities. Being involved in gangs can harm your studies and make it difficult to make real friends outside the gang.

Being in a gang is not the glamorous life movies and television shows sometimes make it out to be. It is actually a violent life that ends too early for many gang members.

Work It Out

1. Make friends outside of gangs. It may seem cool to be part of a group of kids who stick together and are loyal to each other. But you are better off developing real friends, not kids who are forced to bond with you.

2. Don't give in to the pressure. If you feel pressured to join a gang, it can be helpful to talk with people who are not involved in gangs or quit a gang. School counselors are also great people to turn to if you need help.

3. Get connected, stay active, and focus on education, summer programs, and other positive and productive activities.

The Last Word from Ryan

For many guys, there is something appealing about being part of a gang that will accept you for who you are. But the truth is that you don't need to be part of a gang to make that happen. Just stay true to yourself. Eventually, you will make trustworthy, loyal friends without the help—and problems—of gangs.

Friends play an important role in our lives. They make our lives more fun and interesting. Experts say having friends is critical for your mental and emotional well-being and your social development. They even help you to be a better student. Friendships become especially important when you get to be an adolescent. That's why it can seem so difficult for you to deal with your social life sometimes.

Being an adult means I rarely have to deal with any drama from friends. Unfortunately, that was seldom the case when I was your age. Psychologists who have studied friendships say that little kids develop very intense friendships and are extremely loyal toward each other. As they grow up, their friendships become more complex and layered.

So, you see, the problems you are having—or are about to have—are normal. These conflicts are a part of growing up. They just happen to intensify during adolescence, when we are all so vulnerable and inconsistent in our attitudes and behavior. When I was in middle school, I got into numerous fights and nasty arguments with other kids. Now, many of those guys are my close friends.

I know the issues discussed in this book can leave you feeling distraught. I also know you probably don't want to share those emotions. Few guys do. I hope reading this book helps you deal with them. My goal was to remind you that you are not alone in dealing with your emotions and challenges. Almost every guy goes through struggles with classmates, teammates, and friends. So, learn from what my friends and I have experienced. One day, you will have several longtime, loyal friends, too.

Good luck!

Ryan

Pay It Forward

Remember, a healthful life is about balance. Now that you know how to walk that path, pay it forward to a friend or even yourself! Remember the Work It Out tips throughout this book, and then take these steps to get healthy and get going.

- Reach out to loners, new kids, and other guys who need friends. They will be grateful for your interest. It could mean the start of a new friendship.

- Look for other kids who share your interests. Sharing interests such as sports, music, and theater helps guys bond. You will always have things to do together and things you can talk about.

- Stay true to yourself. It can be difficult to avoid getting wrapped up in fads and other social trends. But if you act like yourself, you will have an easier time making good friends.

- Do not tolerate bullying as the victim or a bystander. Bullying only harms people, even the bully himself. Remember, being a witness to bullying can also hurt you emotionally. Speak up.

- Be a loyal, forgiving friend. Stand by the people you trust, and they will stand by you. Forgive your friends when they hurt you. You will want them to forgive you when you make a mistake. Friendships are bound to involve conflict. Grow and learn from these conflicts.

- Stay in touch with friends who move away. With the Internet and other technological advances, it's easier to do so. If you value a friendship, you don't have to end it just because you don't see your friend as often.

- Avoid gangs. Find real friends who will look out for you.

- Learn about new cultures. Be open and accepting of guys from different cultures. It's amazing what you will learn.

- Above all, be who you are. Be confident and proud. Be with people who make you feel good.

Additional Resources

Selected Bibliography

Haber, Joel David. *Bullyproof Your Child for Life: Protect Your Child from Teasing, Taunting, and Bullying for Good.* New York: Perigee, 2007.

Marcus, Dave. *What It Takes to Pull Me Through: Why Teenagers Get in Trouble—And How Four of Them Got Out.* Boston, MA: Houghton Mifflin, 2005.

Sheras, Peter L. *Your Child: Bully or Victim? Understanding and Ending Schoolyard Tyranny.* New York: Fireside, 2002.

Further Reading

Clément, Claude, and Melissa Daly. *Don't Be Shy: How to Fit In, Make Friends, and Have Fun—Even If You Weren't Born Outgoing.* New York: Amulet, 2005.

Desetta, Al, ed. *The Courage to Be Yourself: True Stories by Teens About Cliques, Conflicts, and Overcoming Peer Pressure.* Minneapolis, MN: Free Spirit, 2005.

Humphrey, Sandra McLeod. *Hot Issues, Cool Choices: Facing Bullies, Peer Pressure, Popularity and Put-downs.* Amherst, NY: Prometheus, 2007.

Web Sites

To learn more about dealing with friends and enemies, visit ABDO Publishing Company online at **www.abdopublishing.com**. Web sites about dealing with friends and enemies are featured on our Book Links page. These links are routinely monitored and updated to provide the most current information available.

For More Information

For more information on this subject, contact or visit the following organizations:

Big Brothers Big Sisters of America
230 North 13th Street
Philadelphia, PA 19107
215-567-7000
www.bbbs.org
Volunteers are connected to youth ages 6 to 18 to create a mentoring relationship in which all kinds of activities can happen.

Boy Scouts of America
www.scouting.org
Boy Scouts of America provides a program for young people to build character, get trained in the responsibilities of participating citizenship, and develop personal fitness.

National Center for Bullying Prevention
PACER Center, Inc.
8161 Normandale Boulevard
Bloomington, MN 55437
888-248-0822
www.pacerkidsagainstbullying.org
The center provides information about how to counter and deal with bullying.

Glossary

abandon
> To desert or leave somebody alone who you used to care about.

alienated
> Feeling apart and different from people around you.

anxious
> Feeling nervous and hyper.

brotherhood
> A tight bond between guys who are similar to each other, almost as though they are really brothers.

clique
> A tight group of friends who often exclude others from their group.

discipline
> The ability to control your actions even under tough circumstances.

dominance
> Control and power over somebody else.

drama
> Emotional circumstances; commotion between people.

exclude
> To prevent somebody from joining in.

fad

A quirky trend or style that usually does not last long.

humiliated

Embarrassed to an extreme level.

impressionable

Able to be influenced by others; vulnerable.

loyalty

Standing by your friends and family, even in tough situations.

mature

Grown up; acting more like an adult than a kid.

phase

A period of time when a person acts in a way that is unlike them.

validate

To confirm; endorse somebody else's ideas.

Index

HURON PUBLIC LIBRARY
521 DAKOTA AVE S
HURON, SD 57350

About the Author

Ryan Basen is a writer and journalism professor living in Charlotte, North Carolina. A former newspaper and magazine reporter, Ryan has also written books about NBA and NASCAR stars and sports issues. He earned awards from the North Carolina Press Association and Associated Press Sports Editors for work he did as a reporter with *The Charlotte Observer* newspaper in 2007 and 2008.

Photo Credits

iStockphoto, cover, 3, 71, 97; James Pauls/iStockphoto, 12; Alan Crosthwaite/iStockphoto, 16; Lori Sparkia/iStockphoto, 22; Duncan Walker/iStockphoto, 25; Skip Odonnell/iStockphoto, 26; Chris Schmidt/iStockphoto, 32; Cat London/iStockphoto, 34; Patrick Herrera/iStockphoto, 36; Arthur Kwiatkowski/iStockphoto, 41; Matty Symons/iStockphoto, 44; Courtney Navey/iStockphoto, 49; Tova Teitelbaum/iStockphoto, 50; Julián Rovagnati/iStockphoto, 52; Gautier Willaume/iStockphoto, 54; Derek Latta/iStockPhoto, 61; Justin Horrocks/iStockphoto, 63; Hillary Fox/iStockphoto, 65; Cathleen Abers-Kimball/iStockphoto, 69; Arthur Kwiatkowski/iStockphoto, 72; Kristian Sekulic/iStockphoto, 77; Denise Kappa/iStockphoto, 79; Yuriy Kirsanov/iStockphoto, 86; Wilson Valentin/iStockphoto, 89; Denis Jr. Tangney/iStockphoto, 95

HURON PUBLIC LIBRARY
521 DAKOTA AVE S
HURON, SD 57350